First World War
and Army of Occupation
War Diary
France, Belgium and Germany

25 DIVISION
75 Infantry Brigade
Royal Warwickshire Regiment
1/8th Territorial Battalion
1 September 1918 - 28 February 1919

WO95/2251/4

The Naval & Military Press Ltd
www.nmarchive.com
Published in association with The National Archives

Published by

The Naval & Military Press Ltd

Unit 10 Ridgewood Industrial Park,

Uckfield, East Sussex,

TN22 5QE England

Tel: +44 (0) 1825 749494

www.naval-military-press.com

www.nmarchive.com

This diary has been reprinted in facsimile from the original. Any imperfections are inevitably reproduced and the quality may fall short of modern type and cartographic standards.

© **Crown Copyright**
Images reproduced by permission of The National Archives, London, England, 2015.

Contents

Document type	Place/Title	Date From	Date To
Heading	WO95/2251-4		
Heading	8th Bn Royal Warwick Regt Sep 1918-Feb 1919		
War Diary	Asiago Plateau	01/09/1918	11/09/1918
War Diary	Centrale Italy	12/09/1918	18/09/1918
War Diary	France	19/09/1918	20/09/1918
War Diary	Yvrencheux	21/09/1918	21/09/1918
War Diary	Cramont	23/09/1918	30/09/1918
Heading	War Diary Of 1/8th Bn The Royal Warwickshire Regt. 1st October 1918 to 31st October 1918		
Miscellaneous	74th Bde Diary		
War Diary	Combles (Somme)	01/10/1918	02/10/1918
War Diary	Nurlu	03/10/1918	03/10/1918
War Diary	Guinnemont FM	04/10/1918	05/10/1918
War Diary	Lormisett	06/10/1918	12/10/1918
War Diary	Serain	13/10/1918	16/10/1918
War Diary	Honnechy	17/10/1918	22/10/1918
War Diary	Pommereuil	23/10/1918	23/10/1918
War Diary	Flaquet Brifaut	24/10/1918	24/10/1918
War Diary	Pommereuil	25/10/1918	31/10/1918
War Diary	Le Faux	01/11/1918	03/11/1918
War Diary	Landrecies	04/11/1918	04/11/1918
War Diary	Maroilles	05/11/1918	07/11/1918
War Diary	Marbaix	08/11/1918	08/11/1918
War Diary	Preux-Au-Bois	09/11/1918	12/11/1918
War Diary	Le Cateau	13/11/1918	30/11/1918
Miscellaneous	75th Inf Bde	05/01/1918	05/01/1918
War Diary	Carnieres	01/12/1918	16/12/1918
War Diary	Cambrai	17/12/1918	28/02/1919

WO 95/22511/4.

25TH DIVISION
75TH INFY BDE

8TH BN ROYAL WARWICK REGT
SEP 1918 - FEB 1919

(FROM 48 DIV.
143 Bde ITALY)

and France 1915 MAR - 1917 OCT
Same Division

WAR DIARY
or
INTELLIGENCE SUMMARY.
(Erase heading not required.)

Army Form C. 2118.

Ref. Tra BRENTA PIAVE 1/50000
ABBEVILLE 1/100000

Place	Date	Hour	Summary of Events and Information	Remarks and references to Appendices
ASIAGO PLATEAU.	1/9/18		The Battalion was holding the B/F sector of the right Bde front of the British line in Italy. The day was quiet. Infantries unchanged.	
	2.			
	3.		No change in positions. Our patrols were active during the night but on neither occasion established contact with the enemy.	
	4.		Situation generally quiet.	
	5.		Our artillery was rather active otherwise everything was quiet.	
	6.		The Battalion was relieved by the 1st + 7th R. War. R. on the line and moved into the support battalion area.	
	7.		The unit finished working parties + outposts.	
	8.		Officers carried out reconnaissance schemes in the support area the usual working parties were found.	
	9.		The Bn Coy of GRANEZZA were relieving 6th Battalion and the companies tilted in turn.	
	10.		The 1/5 + 8th Worcesters Rg't relieved the battalion and an relief companies marched independently to GRANEZZA camp.	
	11		The day was devoted to cleaning up and reorganisation orders were received ordering the unit to move down to the plains and the troops rode transported by lorries to CENTRALE.	
CENTRALE 2. ITALY.	13		The entraining orders were received but was cancelled and cattle unit remained at CENTRALE.	
	14.		The unit entrained for FRANCE and the train having upon which the battalion was transported moved by the Riviera route.	
	15.			
	16.			
	17.			
	18.			
FRANCE	19.		The journey occupied to depart'd the 19th when the battalion arrived at ST RIQUIER and detrained there and marched to VACQUEUX. The battalion remained at this village for the day.	
	20.			

Army Form C. 2118.

WAR DIARY
or
INTELLIGENCE SUMMARY.
(Erase heading not required.)

Instructions regarding War Diaries and Intelligence Summaries are contained in F. S. Regs., Part II. and the Staff Manual respectively. Title pages will be prepared in manuscript.

Place	Date	Hour	Summary of Events and Information	Remarks and references to Appendices
VIBERCHEUX	21/8/18		Orders were received to move to CRAMONT and the battalion marched there.	ap
CRAMONT	23		Training commenced. Guns Sun were being a special feature.	ap
	24		Training.	ap
	25		Training during the morning. Ruminational training during the afternoon.	ap
	26		The battalion was inspected by the Brigadier.	ap
	27		The unit entrained at ST RIQUIER for the forward area and detrained at ALBERT and marched to billets at WARLOY.	ap
	28		Rested this day.	ap
	29		The battalion was moved in lorries to MONTAUBAN and rested there.	ap
	30		The day was spent in training and preparation for the move on the following day.	ap

Lt Col
Commanding
8th Loyal R

D. D. & L., London, E.C.
(A5001) Wt. W1771/M2031 750,000 5/17 Sch. 53 Forms/C2118/14

WAR DIARY

OF

16th Bn. The Royal Warwickshire Regt.

From 1st October, 1918
To 31st October, 1918.

Wrong dates - for 6:
read 5: See 74" Bde diary

[signature]

2/2/37.

Army Form C. 2118.

WAR DIARY
or
INTELLIGENCE SUMMARY.
(Erase heading not required.)

Ref Maps LENS 11
ST QUENTIN
VALENCIENNES

Instructions regarding War Diaries and Intelligence Summaries are contained in F. S. Regs, Part II. and the Staff Manual respectively. Title pages will be prepared in manuscript.

Place	Date	Hour	Summary of Events and Information	Remarks and references to Appendices
COMBLES (SUNNIE)	1		The battalion was moving up to the battle front and rested here this day	
	2		Orders were received which caused the battalion to march to NURLU and the battalion moved in accordance.	
NURLU	3		Operation orders ordering the battalion to proceed to the STEPHIGE area received and the battalion arrived there at 9.30pm and rested in a field there.	
GUINNEMONT FM	4		O.O. No 5 ordering the unit to GUINNEMONT farm was received and the battalion marched there and rested for a few hours in the trenches in the vicinity.	
	5		At 02.30 the battalion marched with the line at LORMISETT to support the 74 "N.Y." of Bde.	
LORMISETT.	6		A + C. Coys were ordered to support the SHERWOOD FORESTERS in the vicinity of GUISANCOURT farm and to assist them in the attack of this rallying point. B + D Coys moved to support the Yorks Regt at BELLEVILLE farm. The advance of the companies under Heavy Artillery and M.G fire was support and the G.O.C. the 74th Bde complimented Lt Colonel Whitehouse on the splendid way in which the advance was carried out.	
	7		A + C Coys assisted the SHERWOOD FORESTERS to Capture GUISANCOURT FARM, the work of 2nd Lt W.G. Brown and a platoon of C. Coy which captured a key position here made the remainder of the attack simple. Dispositions of A + C Coys remained unchanged D Coy went off to support the 1/8 WORCESTERS with Head Quarters at BEAUREVOIR while B Coy returned to LORMISETT and eventually was under the command of Colonel Whitehouse again.	

WAR DIARY
or
INTELLIGENCE SUMMARY.
(Erase heading not required.)

Army Form C. 2118.

Place	Date	Hour	Summary of Events and Information	Remarks and references to Appendices
LORMISETT	Oct 7		On the line being reorganised the whole battalion returned to LORMISETT and was over night under command of the C.O.	
	8.		The success of the operations of this day brought the battalion into action at SONIA from where it held a gap between the 30th American Div and our 4th Bde. At 22.05 hrs orders to resume the attack were received and the battalion moved up to the forming up position between SERAIN and PREMONT.	
	9.		Zero was at 5.20 and at this hour the battalion advanced and took its objective beyond MARETZ by 06.30 hrs. The battalion rested in this area during the day but held orders for the resumption of the attack came and the battalion moved.	
	10		Starting from a point N. of HONNECHY with ZERO at 5.30 the battalion advanced after heavy fighting to the outskirts of LE CATEAU and here owing to the fact that the Americans on the right had been held up further advance became impossible. The positions taken were consolidated and held.	
	11		The line was taken over this day by the 50th Div and the battalion marched out to HONNECHY. This was the end of what was probably the heaviest most continuous fighting which the battalion had met and the battalion came out with fresh laurels added to its reputation. The casualties during the battle were 1 officer 24 O.R. killed 5 officers 168 O.R. wounded. The battalion moved to SERAIN to rest.	

WAR DIARY or INTELLIGENCE SUMMARY.

Army Form C. 2118.

Ref Map 57B

Place	Date	Hour	Summary of Events and Information	Remarks and references to Appendices
SERAIN	13/10/18		Sunday. Voluntary services were held for troops of all denominations.	
	14/10/18		Brig. Genl. Hungell D.S.O. commanding the Brigade inspected the battalion and complimented all ranks on the achievements of the strenuous fighting of the previous week. Reorganization and re-equipment of the battalion commenced.	
	15.		The work of reorganizing the battalion continued and training was started.	
	16.		As the Brigade was ordered to be in reserve to the 50th Division for their attack on the German line along the R. SELLE the battalion moved to HONNECHY.	
HONNECHY.	17		At 12.00 hours the order to move to Q19 Central was received and the unit moved in accordance.	
	18		At 9.30 hours the Brigade continued the attack commanded by the 50th Div and the battalion was in support to the WORCESTERS + GLOSTERS who led the attack. As the attack developed D Coy was sent up to reinforce the WORCESTERS. C. Coy were sent up to the WORCESTERS while A+B Coys remained in support along the road at R.19.a. C + D. Coys moved with the WORCESTERS to the attack on BASUEL which was taken and held.	
	19		Dispositions of Coys remained unchanged HQ moved to R 184.7. D. Coy was withdrawn from the WORCESTERS and joined A+B Coys at RIQ.a. at 20.30hrs	
	20.		The battalion was relieved and marched out to ST BENN. Casualties during the tour. 3 OR. KILLED 27. OR. WOUNDED. Here the unit rested and reorganised.	
	21			
	22.		In the evening of this day the battalion which had been attached to the 7th Bde for the attack on the RICHEMONT line moved up to its position along the railway in R.2. etc	

WAR DIARY
or
INTELLIGENCE SUMMARY.
(Erase heading not required.)

Army Form C. 2118.

Place	Date	Hour	Summary of Events and Information	Remarks and references to Appendices
POMMEREUIL.	23/10/18		The attack commenced at 01.20 hours the battalion moving in rear of the 9th DEVONS and the battalion was to be used to help to mop up POMMEREUIL if necessary or if this necessity did not arise to pass through the 7th Bde and carry the intermediate objective which was the road in L.22.a7d. Owing to haze the attacking units of the first wave became rather mixed up and the situation was for some time rather obscure but Capt M. Mortimore. M.C.(who was commanding the battalion at this time) going out and taking command of troops of all units and organising attacks on enemy M.Guns which had been missed by the forward during the fog, the situation rapidly cleared and all objectives were gained. The 7th Bde continued the attack through the BOIS L'EVEQUE and the battalion was ordered to concentrate in the vicinity of FLAQUET BRIANT on L.15.d. This move was completed by 10.53.p. and the battalion remained here until units of the 9th Bde passed through our time to enquire the unit marched out to billets in POMMEREUIL. The casualties during the day were KILLED 1/3 OR. WOUNDED OFFICERS 3 OR. 40. MISSING 5 OR. The work of reorganisation was commenced at once and a draft of 14 SOR. was absorbed.	
FLAQUET BRIANT.	24			
POMMEREUIL.	25			
	27		Training was carried out under company arrangements the O.C. and company officers made a reconnaissance of the forward area in the vicinity of FONTAINE au BOIS in preparation for a further ordered operation to be carried out by the battalion.	
	28		Training & re organisation continued	
	29		" "	
	30		The companies continued training and the men bathed during the day	
	31.		The battalion relieved the 11th Sherwood Foresters in the Right Sector of the Divisional Front.	

WAR DIARY
INTELLIGENCE SUMMARY

Army Form C. 2118.

1/6 R Warwick Regt

Ref. Sheet 57b 1/40,000, 57a 1/40,000

Place	Date	Hour	Summary of Events and Information	Remarks and references to Appendices
LE FAUX	1/11/18		The battalion was holding the Regt sector of the Divisional front with C. Coy on the right, D. Coy on the left, B in support and A Coy counter attack company	All
	2		Dispositions remained unchanged and the day was quiet; there was a little patrol activity at night.	All
	3		Owing to the rainy weather the forward companies were relieved A Coy taking over the right and B Coy the left. The day was uneventful	All
LANDRECIES	4	06.05	The battalion attacked and after a very severe fight secured its objective astride the line of the river SAMBRE at LANDRECIES establishing a bridgehead there at M17c6.3. Orders were received from Bde at 15.40 hours which ordered the battalion to concentrate in the area G2h2 and the battalion moved in accordance with these orders.	All
	5		The battalion received orders to continue the advance and to protect the right flank of the 74th Infy Bde which was attacking the line of the PETIT HELPE river. The battalion moved along the LANDRECIES-MAROILLES road in the order A.B.C.D. companies and advanced without opposition until the leading company came under fire from the outskirts of MAROILLES. At 19.15 hours the Division operating on our right (which had been held up by the fire of hostile machine guns) came up into line with the 74th Inf Bde and this relieved the battalion of its duty as flank guard. Companies were billeted in houses along the LANDRECIES-MAROILLES rd and rested there the day.	All
MAROILLES	6		No change	
	7	00.21	ordering the battalion to continue the advance resumed. The orders to resume the advance detailed the battalion to act as part of the main guard and the outpost line was passed at 10.15 hours and the advance continued from the Eastern outskirts of MARBAIX to the village of ST HILAIRE aux HELPS where the vanguard was engaged by enemy M.G. posts. The main guard was not involved and the battalion was relieved at 22.00 hours by the CONNAUGHT RANGERS and marched out to billets in MARBAIX. The casualties during this period of action were 1 officer and 29 O.R. killed 2 officers " 106 O.R. Wounded	All

45.W
Rouen

1/8 R. Warwick Regt.

Army Form C. 2118.

WAR DIARY
or
INTELLIGENCE SUMMARY.
(Erase heading not required.)

Instructions regarding War Diaries and Intelligence Summaries are contained in F. S. Regs., Part II. and the Staff Manual respectively. Title pages will be prepared in manuscript.

Place	Date	Hour	Summary of Events and Information	Remarks and references to Appendices
MARBAIX.	8/11/18		The battalion marched out to the rest area at PREUX-AU-BOIS via LANDRECIES.	All
PREUX-AU-BOIS	9/11/18		The day was directed to cleaning of equipment and billets and reorganisation.	All
	10		Companies commenced training under company arrangements. The afternoon was devoted to recreational training.	All
	11		Battalion drill was a prominent feature of the training. Strength including the unit moved from PREUX and test and bathed from 10.00 hrs to 12.00 hrs.	All
	12		The unit moved from PREUX parade	All
LE CATEAU	13.		Training continued during the morning and the afternoon was spent in recreation.	All
	14		Training	All
	15.		Divine Services were held for troops of all denominations.	All
	16.		Training	All
	17		Battalion route march was carried out. The route was REUMONT- HONNECHY - BUSIGNY - LE CATEAU.	All
	18		A + B Coys carried out salvage operations in the area W/LE CATEAU. C + D Coys trained under Company arrangements	All
	19		Work and training as on the 19th inst. Musketry was a special feature of the training.	All
	20		C + D Coys carried out salvage work and A + B Coys trained.	All
	21		All denominations attended Divine Service. The C.E. service was a parade service held at the Theatre	All
	22.		A + B Coys continued salvage operations. C + D Coys trained at the Divisional Baths.	All
	23		Ditto	All
	24		Ditto C + D Coys carried out training	All
	25.			All
	26		Ditto	All
	27		C + D. Coys worked in the area. tote relieved A+B Coys	All
	28		The battalion moved from LE CATEAU to CARNIERES.	All
	29		From 09.00 to 10.00 hrs there was a ceremonial parade; the battalion marched past the commanding officer.	All
	30		The remainder of the morning was devoted to kit inspections and the cleaning of billets.	All

75th Inf Bde

Herewith Original
& Copy of War Diary for
month of December 1918.

[signature]

C296
5/1/919
Lieut Colonel
Commdg 1/8th R War R

ORIGINAL

Army Form C. 2118.

1/8th Bn
The Royal Warwickshire Regt

WAR DIARY
or
INTELLIGENCE SUMMARY.
(Erase heading not required.)

46.W
(3 sheets)

VOL 46

Place	Date	Hour	Summary of Events and Information	Remarks and references to Appendices
CARNIERES	1918 Dec. 1		Divine Service.	C/O
	2		2 Companies :- Drill & 2 Companies :- Salvage work.	C/P
	3		do.	C/P
	4		Battalion parade for ceremonial Drill. Visit of H.M. The King.	C/P
	5		Bathing at AVESNES LES AUBERT. Fumigation of Blankets.	C/P
	6		2 Companies :- Drill & 2 Companies :- Salvage work	C/P
	7		do. Presentation of Ribands by Div. Commander. C/P	
	8		Divine Service.	
	9		2 Companies :- Drill & 2 Companies :- Salvage work. Presentation of Ribands by Div. Commander.	C/P
	10		2 Companies :- Drill & 2 Companies :- Salvage work.	C/P
	11		Salvage work by whole Battalion.	C/P
	12		Battalion parade for ceremonial drill followed by Company training.	C/P
	13		Salvage work by whole Battalion. Medical inspection of 2 Coys.	C/P
	14		Battalion parade for ceremonial drill followed by Company training.	C/P
	15		Divine Service.	C/P
	16		Battalion moved to CAMBRAI.	C/P
CAMBRAI	17		Training under Company arrangements.	C/P
	18		Battalion parade followed by Company training. Reconnaissance of Salvage area by Company Commanders.	C/P

Army Form C. 2118.

WAR DIARY
or
INTELLIGENCE SUMMARY.
(Erase heading not required.)

1/8th Bn. The Royal Warwickshire Regt

Place	Date 1918	Hour	Summary of Events and Information	Remarks and references to Appendices
CAMBRAI	Dec. 19		Battalion drill followed by Company Training.	CYP
	20		Battalion commenced Salvage operations in new area.	CYP
	21		Battalion drill followed by Company training	CYP
	22		Divine Services & Bathing	CYP
	23		Battalion drill followed by Company training.	CYP
	24		Coy parades or working parties.	CYP
	25		Divine Service in Bôle Cinema. 30 men per Coy attended.	CYP
	26		Coy parades or working parties.	CYP
	27		Battalion drill followed by Company training.	CYP
	28		Training under Company arrangements. Rehearsal of ceremony "Trooping the Colours".	CYP
	29		Divine Services.	CYP
	30		Battalion parade for ceremonial drill	CYP
	31		Trooping the Colours. Reviewing Officer, Major Genl. J.R.E. CHARLES, C.B. D.S.O.	CYP

1/5 R War Regt

47. W.
(2 sheets)

M147

WAR DIARY
or
INTELLIGENCE SUMMARY.
(Erase heading not required.)

Army Form C. 2118.

Instructions regarding War Diaries and Intelligence Summaries are contained in F.S. Regs., Part II. and the Staff Manual respectively. Title pages will be prepared in manuscript.

Place	Date 1919	Hour	Summary of Events and Information	Remarks and references to Appendices
Cambrai	Jan 1		The Battalion carried out Salvage Operations. Education.	C/P
"	2		The Divisional Baths allotted to the Battalion.	C/P
"	3		Salvage Operations and Education.	C/P
"	4		Training under Company Commanders arrangements (2 hrs). Route March (1½ hr) and Education.	C/P
"	5		Divine Services.	C/P
"	6		Salvage Operations and Education	C/P
"	7		Salvage Operations and Education.	C/P
"	8		Route March under Company Commanders arrangements. Platoon Football match.	C/P
"	9		Salvage Operations and Education.	C/P
"	10		Salvage Operations and Education	C/P
"	11		The Divisional Baths allotted to the Battalion. Lantern Lecture.	C/P
"	12		Divine Service.	C/P
"	13		Salvage Operations and Education.	C/P
"	14		Two Companies – Salvage Operations. Two Companies – Training and Education. Football (3rd Round) 25th Divisional Cup. 1/5 R War R. v. 25th Vet M.G. Bn. Result 1/5 Warwick. 3 goals. Div M.G. Bn. 1 goal.	C/P
"	15		Two Companies – Salvage Operations. Two Companies – Training and Education	C/P
"	16		Two Companies – Salvage Operations. Two Companies – Training and Education	C/P
"	17		Two Companies – Salvage Operations. Two Companies – Training and Education	C/P
"	18		Two Companies – Salvage Operations. Two Companies – Training and Education. Football (2nd Round) 25th Divisional Cup. 1/5 R War R. v. 9 Bn. Yorks. Played at Englefontaine. (Result Welsh's 3 goals. 9th Bn. Yorks. 1 goal.) 25th Divisional But. (Semi-final) 1/5th R. Warwick R. v. 21st Manchesters. Result. 1/5th R.W.R. 6 goals. 21st Manchesters. Nil.	C/P
"	19		Divine Services.	C/P
"	20		Two Companies – Salvage Operations. Two Companies – Training and Education.	C/P
"	21		Two Companies – Salvage Operations. Two Companies – Training and Education. 25th Divisional Band Concert.	C/P

Army Form C. 2118.

WAR DIARY
or
INTELLIGENCE SUMMARY.
(Erase heading not required.)

Instructions regarding War Diaries and Intelligence Summaries are contained in F. S. Regs., Part II. and the Staff Manual respectively. Title pages will be prepared in manuscript.

Place	Date 1919	Hour	Summary of Events and Information	Remarks and references to Appendices
Carvin	JAN 22		Nil Training. Salvage operations & Education. The Battalion Fed H.M.C. Team Played the 112 Bde. R.F.A.	O/P
			in the Final of the 25th Divisional Cup at AVESNES-LES-AUBERT. Result - 112 Bde. R.F.A. 4 goals.	O/P
			1/8 R.War.R - 2 goals.	O/P
"	23		The Divisional Baths allotted to the Battalion. Education	O/P
"	24		Two Companies - Salvage Operations. Two Companies - Training and Education	O/P
"	25		Two Companies - Salvage Operations. Two Companies - Training and Education	O/P
"	26		Divine Service	O/P
"	27		Two Companies - Salvage Operations. Two Companies - Training and Education	O/P
			Lecture - Subject "Demobilization and Reconstruction"	
"	28		Two Companies Salvage Operations. Two Companies Training and Education	O/P
"	29		Two Companies Salvage Operations. Two Companies Training and Education	O/P
"	30		Two Companies Salvage Operations. Two Companies Training and Education	O/P
"	31		Two Companies Salvage Operations. Two Companies Training and Education	O/P

Wilhers
Lieut Colonel
Commdg. 1/8 Bn. R. Warwickshire Regt.

WAR DIARY
or
INTELLIGENCE SUMMARY.
(Erase heading not required.)

Army Form C. 2118.

1/8 West Rgt

Place	Date	Hour	Summary of Events and Information	Remarks and references to Appendices
	FEB.			
Cambrai	1		The Divisional Bath allotted to the Battalion. Education.	CP
"	2		Divine Service	CP
"	3		Two Companies - Education and Training. Two Companies Salvage Operations.	CP
"	4		Two Companies - Education and Training. Two Companies Salvage Operations.	CP
"	5		Two Companies - Education and Training. Two Companies Salvage Operations.	CP
"	6		Lecture - Subject "South Africa".	CP
"	7		Recreative Training and Short Route Marches. Education.	CP
"	8		Recreative Training. Shot Route Marches and Education.	CP
"	8		Two Companies Education and Training. Two Companies recreative training, one Platoon forming a Working Party at the Divisional Salvage Dump.	CP
"	9		Inter Platoon Football Competition Final - 5 Platoon v 7 Platoon. result 5 Pltn. 14 - 7 Pltn. 3.	CP
"	9		Lecture. Subject "The New India".	CP
"	9		Divine Service	CP
"	10		Two Companies Education. Training. Two Companies Salvage Operations.	CP
"	11		- Do - Do - Do - Do -	CP
"	12		- Do - Do - Do - Do -	CP

Army Form C. 2118.

WAR DIARY
or
INTELLIGENCE SUMMARY.
(Erase heading not required.)

Instructions regarding War Diaries and Intelligence Summaries are contained in F. S. Regs., Part II. and the Staff Manual respectively. Title pages will be prepared in manuscript.

Place	Date	Hour	Summary of Events and Information	Remarks and references to Appendices
	Feb.			
Cambrai	13		Two Companies Education and Training. Two Companies Salvage Operations	CP
"	14		- " - Do - " - Do -	CP
"	15		The Divisional Bath allotted to the Battalion.	CR
"	16		Divine Service	CP
"	17		Two Companies Education and Training. Two Companies Salvage Operation	CP
			Coy Football Competition 1/8 R. War R. v. 2nd Bn. Bedfordshire Regt. result 1/8 RWR 2 goals 2nd Beds. 2 goals	CR
"	18		Two Companies Education and Training Two Companies Salvage Operations	CP
"	19		- " - Do - " - Do -	CP
"	20		- " - Do - " - Do -	CP
"	21		- " - Do - " - Do -	CP
"	22		- " - Do - " - Do -	CP
"	23		Divine Service	CP
"	24		Two Companies Education & Training Two Companies Salvage Operations	CP
"	25		All Companies were at the disposal of Company Commanders (2 hours).	CP
			The Commanding Officer inspected the Battalion.	CR
"	26		The Divisional Baths allotted to the Battalion	CP

Army Form C. 2118.

WAR DIARY
or
INTELLIGENCE SUMMARY.
(Erase heading not required.)

Place	Date	Hour	Summary of Events and Information	Remarks and references to Appendices
Camiers	Feb. 27		All Companies at the disposal of Company Commanders	CTP
"	28		200 O.Rs. proceeded to join the 2/6th Bn. R. Warwick R. at Havre	CTP
"			206 O.Rs. proceeded to join the 2/7th Bn. R. Warwick R. at Etaples	CTP
			During the month of February 282 O.Rs. left this Unit for Dispersal Centres pending demobilisation.	CTP.

5/3/1919

[signature]
Major
Commanding
1/6 R. Warwick R.

www.ingramcontent.com/pod-product-compliance
Lightning Source LLC
Chambersburg PA
CBHW081508160426
43193CB00014B/2621